TRAVEL WITH THE GREAT EXPLORERS

Explore with

Henry Hudson

Tim Cooke

Crabtree Publishing Company

www.crabtreebooks.com

Crabtree Publishing Company

www.crabtreebooks.com

Author: Tim Cooke
Publishing plan research and development:
  Reagan Miller
Managing editor: Tim Cooke
Editorial director: Lindsey Lowe
Editors: Kelly Spence, Natalie Hyde
Proofreader: Kathy Middleton
Designer: Lynne Lennon
Picture manager: Sophie Mortimer
Design manager: Keith Davis
Children's publisher: Anne O'Daly
**Production coordinator
  and prepress technican:** Tammy McGarr
Print coordinator: Margaret Amy Salter

Produced by Brown Bear Books for
  Crabtree Publishing Company

Photographs:
Front Cover:
Alamy: North Wind Picture Archives main, tr, cr;
Shutterstock: br.

Interior:
Alamy: Interfoto 21b, Mary Evans Picture Library 15b, North
Wind Picture 8, 12, 20-21, 26, Pictorial Press Ltd 25:
Bridgeman Art Library: Peter Newark Pictorial Pictures 29,
Private Collection 15t; **Dreamstime:** 6, 7, 9t; 12b, 22t; **istock-
photo:** 7b. 16tr. 26cl, 26-27; **Mary Evans Picture Library:** 14;
Public Domain: 28t, Sifting the Past 11tr; **Robert Hunt Library:**
10; **Shutterstock:** 17b, Victor Kiev 29l, Spirit of America 13,
23t. Gary Whitton 23t: **Thinkstock:** istockphoto 8-9,
Photos.com 17cl; **Topfoto:** The Granger Collection 11bl, 12-13,
16, 18, 19, 24, 27, 28b, The National Archives/Heritage Images
21t, Charles Walker 22b:

Library and Archives Canada Cataloguing in Publication

Cooke, Tim, 1961-, author
      Explore with Henry Hudson / Tim Cooke.

(Travel with the great explorers)
Includes index.
Issued in print and electronic formats.
ISBN 978-0-7787-1246-6 (bound).--ISBN 978-0-7787-1258-9 (pbk.).--
ISBN 978-1-4271-7573-1 (pdf).--ISBN 978-1-4271-7569-4 (html)

      1. Hudson, Henry, -1611--Juvenile literature. 2. Explorers--
Canada--Biography--Juvenile literature. 3. Explorers--Great
Britain--Biography--Juvenile literature. 4. Canada--Discovery and
exploration--British--Juvenile literature. 5. Northwest Passage--
Discovery and exploration--British--Juvenile literature. I. Title.

FC3211.1.H8C66 2014   j971.01'14092   C2013-908703-6
                                                 C2013-908704-4

Library of Congress Cataloging-in-Publication Data

Cooke, Tim, 1961-
  Explore with Henry Hudson / Cooke, Tim.
        pages cm. -- (Travel with the great explorers)
  Includes index.
  ISBN 978-0-7787-1246-6 (reinforced library binding) -- ISBN 978-0-
7787-1258-9 (pbk.) -- ISBN 978-1-4271-7573-1 (electronic pdf) -- ISBN
978-1-4271-7569-4 (electronic html)
  1. Hudson, Henry, -1611--Juvenile literature. 2. Explorers--America--
Biography--Juvenile literature. 3. Explorers--Great Britain--Biography--
Juvenile literature. 4. America--Discovery and exploration--British--
Juvenile literature. I. Title.

  E129.H8C66 2014
  910.92--dc23
  [B]
                                    2013050817

Crabtree Publishing Company

www.crabtreebooks.com 1-800-387-7650

Printed in Canada/022014/MA20131220

**Published in Canada
Crabtree Publishing**
616 Welland Ave.
St. Catharines, ON
L2M 5V6

**Published in the United States
Crabtree Publishing**
PMB 59051
350 Fifth Avenue, 59th Floor
New York, New York 10118

**Published in the United Kingdom
Crabtree Publishing**
Maritime House
Basin Road North, Hove
BN41 1WR

**Published in Australia
Crabtree Publishing**
3 Charles Street
Coburg North
VIC, 3058

CONTENTS

Meet the Boss

No one knows much about explorer Henry Hudson's life. He must have gone to sea at a young age. In 1607, he was ready to lead an expedition north toward the Arctic.

MAN OF MYSTERY

+ Where Did Hudson Get His Sea Legs?

We don't know anything for sure about Henry Hudson's early life. He was likely born around 1565 in England. He may have gone to sea as a boy, so perhaps he came from a family of sailors. By 1607, he was such a good navigator that an English trading company hired him to find a route to Asia by way of the North Pole.

Trade

Hudson was hired to find new trade routes between Europe and Asia. Many other explorers were involved in similar quests.

GO NORTH YOUNG MAN!

☛ **Hudson Latest Traveler in the North Atlantic**

☛ **Follows Long Line of English Explorers**

Henry Hudson was not the first explorer to look for the **Northwest Passage** to Asia. English adventurers had sailed the North Atlantic Ocean for a century hunting for the shortcut. Men such as William Baffin and Martin Frobisher risked the stormy northern waters, but no one found what they were seeking.

DEAD END

- ★ **Hudson Hunts for Northeast Passage**
- ★ **Driven Back by Harsh Conditions**

Henry Hudson made his first two voyages for the Muscovy Company, an English company with trade links to Russia. The company wanted to find a trade route to Asia. First, Hudson tried to sail north over the North Pole. Then he tried to find the **Northeast Passage** around the top of Russia. Both times, Hudson was stopped by bitterly cold weather, strong winds, and seas full of ice.

> " We saw many birds with black backs and white bellies, in form much like a Duck."
> *Henry Hudson describes seeing penguins.*

My Explorer Journal

★ **Hudson's decision to sail on behalf of the Netherlands was very controversial. Both the English and the Dutch were fighting to increase their trade in the world. Was Hudson right or wrong to sail for another country? Give reasons for your decision.**

TREACHERY!

- **+ Navigator Betrays his Country**
- **+ English King Hopping Mad**

After his two failed voyages, the Muscovy Company fired Hudson. In 1609, the Dutch East India Company paid him to look for the Northeast Passage again. The voyage was so cold that Hudson turned around, but this time he sailed to North America. He explored the east coast and claimed land for the Dutch, who were fierce trade competitors of the English. King James I of England was so furious he had Hudson arrested.

Did you know?

Hudson sailed into bays and rivers on the east coast of North America looking for a route to the Pacific Ocean—the legendary Northwest Passage.

Where Are We Heading?

NORTH!

Europeans sought sea routes to trade with Asia because existing land routes were controlled by Muslim countries.

Hudson led four voyages to try to reach the Spice Islands of Asia. They took him into some of the most dangerous seas in the world—and eventually to the frozen bays of what is now northern Canada.

THWARTED—TWICE!

- Expedition Seeks Shortcut to Spices
- Way Blocked by Frozen Islands

Hudson's first voyages were in search of a sea route to Asia. The Northeast Passage was thought to lead around the top of what is now Russia. In 1607, and again in 1608, Hudson's crew tried to find it. The first time they sailed north. The second time they sailed east as far as the Barents Sea. Both times, harsh weather and ice turned them back.

TRAVEL UPDATE

Watch out for ice!

★The legendary Northwest Passage to Asia around the top of North America actually does exist—but it was not traveled until 1906. The fact that the Arctic Ocean is frozen for a good part of the year makes the route of little commercial use. However, in recent years, warmer temperatures mean that the sea routes are open for more of the year.

A DISAPPOINTMENT

★ **A Natural Highway...**

★ **...But Not to the Arctic**

In 1609, Henry Hudson sailed to the New World and into a great bay where the river meets the sea. He hoped the huge waterway might be a **strait** that would lead into the Arctic Ocean and the Northwest Passage. But by the time he had sailed upstream to what is now Albany, he realized he was sailing on a river. Now named for the explorer, the Hudson River flows for 315 miles (505 km) through New York State down to New York Bay.

HUDSON BAY

+ A Sea of Floating Ice

In 1610, on his fourth voyage, Hudson sailed through a narrow stretch of water, now called Hudson Strait, into a huge bay in eastern Canada. The bay, now called Hudson Bay, was full of floating ice that made it like a maze. Hudson could not find a way out to the West. When winter came, his ship was trapped in the ice in the southern branch of the bay called James Bay.

Hudson's Voyages in North America

Henry Hudson made four voyages between 1607 and 1611 in search of a northern sea route to Asia. On his last two voyages, he explored eastern North America—and lost his life doing so.

Greenland

Hudson Bay

Labrador

NORTH ATLANTIC OCEAN

Canada (present-day)

Newfoundland

NORTH AMERICA

Acadia

United States (present-day)

Hudson Bay
Hudson sailed into the bay that now bears his name in August 1610. He hoped it would lead to a Northwest Passage to Asia. Instead, his ship the *Discovery* became trapped when the bay froze during winter.

James Bay
The crew of the *Discovery* spent eight terrible months icebound in James Bay. In spring, the crew rebelled against Hudson's wish to continue exploring. They set him and some companions adrift in a small boat. The castaways were never seen again.

Hudson River
In September 1609, Hudson sailed into what is now New York Bay. He sailed past present-day Manhattan and up the river that is now named for him. On the way, he encountered many of the native people who lived along the river's banks.

SOUTH ATLANTIC OCEAN

Penobscot Bay
Hudson had his first encounter with Native people when he landed at Penobscot Bay in July 1609. One of his crew noted "the people coming aboard showed us great friendship, but we could not trust them."

Scale 250 miles / 400 km

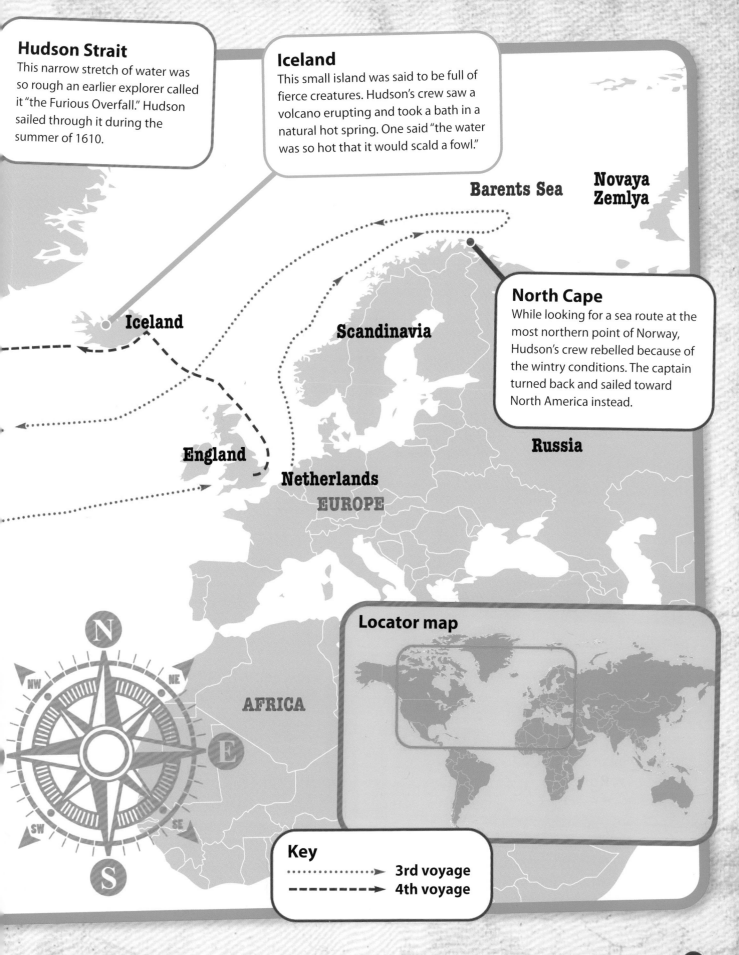

Hudson Strait
This narrow stretch of water was so rough an earlier explorer called it "the Furious Overfall." Hudson sailed through it during the summer of 1610.

Iceland
This small island was said to be full of fierce creatures. Hudson's crew saw a volcano erupting and took a bath in a natural hot spring. One said "the water was so hot that it would scald a fowl."

Barents Sea

Novaya Zemlya

Iceland

Scandinavia

North Cape
While looking for a sea route at the most northern point of Norway, Hudson's crew rebelled because of the wintry conditions. The captain turned back and sailed toward North America instead.

Russia

England

Netherlands

EUROPE

AFRICA

Locator map

Key

............▶ 3rd voyage

– – – – ▶ 4th voyage

Meet the Crew

Hudson's last ship, the *Discovery*, had 25 men and boys onboard. Some had sailed with Hudson before. but that didn't make them loyal. They were among the men who would mutiny against him.

Unreliable Witness

☞ Account by a Spying Servant

☞ Makes Himself Sound Like a Hero

Abacuk Pricket was a servant of Sir Dudley Digges, a nobleman who helped fund the voyage. Pricket may have made the trip so he could report to Digges about it. Pricket wrote the main account of the *Discovery*'s voyage. He says he did not want to join the **mutiny**, but he'd be a fool to say anything else. He's on trial for murder.

DISLOYAL MATE

+ Veteran of Hudson's Early Voyages

+ Leads Rebellion Against his Captain

Robert Juet came from the bustling docks area of London. He had already been Hudson's **mate** on two voyages. But now he was old and cranky—especially since Hudson fired him as mate. Pricket says Juet had already tried to start a mutiny before he joined the real mutiny. But Juet died on the way home, so we only have Pricket's word about his role.

TROUBLEMAKER

★ "Friend" Betrays Captain

Henry Greene was not one of the crew. Pricket wrote, "he was not set down in the owners' book, nor any wages made for him." Pricket says Hudson let Greene live in his home after Greene wasted all his money. On board the *Discovery*, Greene quarreled with everyone. When Hudson didn't give him the coat of a man who died in Canada, Greene began planning his revenge—mutiny!

NOBLE SACRIFICE

+ Ship's Carpenter Has Vital Skills

+ Volunteers for (Almost) Certain Death!

Philip Staffe and Henry Hudson didn't always get along. Staffe was the ship's carpenter, but when Hudson asked him to build a shelter in Canada, Staffe refused. He said he built ships, not houses. But during the mutiny, Staffe asked to be **cast adrift** with the Captain. He probably expected the men would be able to survive until they were rescued. Staffe took his carpenter's chest, full of his valuable tools. He also took a hunting rifle and some gunpowder to shoot birds for food.

Did you know?

A good carpenter was vital on a voyage. He had to be able to repair any damage to the ship and build smaller boats for exploring.

Check Out the Ride

Hudson used three ships on his voyages: the *Hopewell*, *Half Moon*, and the *Discovery*. The ships belonged to his employers, not to him.

All Aboard!

☛ **Right Ship, Wrong Sea**

☛ **Shallow-Water Ship Struggles in Stormy Seas**

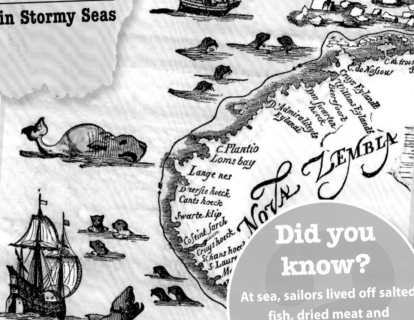

Hudson made his first voyage in the *Hopewell*. It was a pinnace, a sailing ship with three masts. It was quite small, with a crew of just eleven. The *Hopewell* was built for coastal waters, but it must have performed well—Hudson used it again on his second voyage.

HUDSON'S CHOICE

+ More Speed, Less Stability

+ Employers Force Explorer's Hand

The Dutch East India Company gave Hudson the *Halve Maen* (*Half Moon*) for his third voyage. Hudson complained that the ship would be hard to sail. His employers replied, "We can give you no other ship. If you do not want the *Half Moon*, the Company will be obliged to find another Captain to carry out this assignment." Hudson took the job.

Did you know?

At sea, sailors lived off salted fish, dried meat and vegetables, cheese, and beer.

The Floating Palace

- Ship Impresses Native Peoples
- Visit Remembered for Generations

The peoples along the Hudson River had never seen anything like the *Half Moon*. The brightly painted ship dwarfed the canoes they used to paddle out to trade with the crew. For generations, people told stories about the "large house of various colors" on the river.

Shallop

The *Discovery* carried a small, open boat that had oars and sails. Called a shallop, it was used for exploring coasts and for going ashore.

DISCOVERY—NOT!

★ Veteran of Arctic Voyages

★ *Discovery* Fails to Discover

Hudson's last ship was also his largest. It had a crew of 22 men. The *Discovery* was very quick and had a shallow, or flat, bottom, which was good for sailing close to the shore. The *Discovery* had already sailed to the Arctic Ocean under the command of George Weymouth. After Hudson's voyage, the ship made more voyages. In all, the *Discovery* sailed north six times under various captains seeking the Northwest Passage—but it was never successful.

Solve It With Science

Sensation

Read all about the technological advances behind Europe's "golden age" of exploration.

Hudson and his crew sailed at a time when Europeans were getting much better at building ships and navigating, or finding their position.

TECHNO REVOLUTION

- Ship Design Leaps Forward
- Portugal Leads the Way

Most European ships were based on a ship called a carrack, which the Portuguese used for trading. It was large, so it was stable at sea. It had raised sections, called castles, at the front and back for space. Its shallow, or flat, bottom allowed it to sail near coasts. The carrack allowed Portugal and Spain to new land and build huge empires.

DUTCH-MADE
★ A new system for shipbuilding

Shipbuilders usually needed **blueprints** to build a ship, but drawing them up took too long for the Dutch East India Company. It needed ships fast, so it developed a system based on math. Once a shipbuilder knew one measurement of a ship, he used the equations he had memorized to figure out the rest. There was no need to wait for blueprints.

STAR NAVIGATION

★ **A Question of Angles**

★ **I Should Have Tried Harder in Math!**

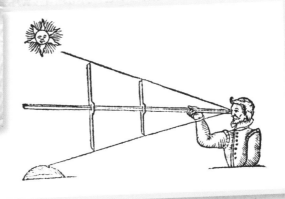

To determine their location, **navigators** used a cross-staff. This was a rod with a crossbar that was used to measure the angle of a heavenly body such as the sun above the **horizon**. A technique called triangulation allowed the navigator to figure out how far north or south he was. But you had to be good at math! On the *Discovery*, Hudson had his own mathematician, Thomas Wydowse.

DEAD RECKONING

+ Easy as Falling Off a Log

The stars could tell sailors how far north or south they were. But to measure how far west they had sailed, sailors needed to measure how fast they were traveling. They dropped a log tied to a rope into the water and measured how much rope was pulled out in a set amount of time to figure out their speed. To make measuring easier, the rope had knots tied into it at regular lengths. Today, the measurement of a ship's speed is still called knots.

Did you know?

Explorers dropped a piece of lead tied to a rope overboard to measure the depth of the sea.

Hanging at Home

Life at sea was hard for all 17th-century sailors. But it was nothing compared to the *Discovery*'s winter in Hudson Bay. The ship became trapped in ice in an inlet called James Bay in November 1610.

Did you know?

Arctic explorers were always concerned that their ships would be crushed by pressure if the ship became icebound. The ice piling up outside a ship was said to make a sound like thunder.

 Weather Forecast

FREEZING WINTER

In James Bay temperatures sank below 0°F (−18°C). The crew built a shelter but the inside walls were coated with ice. They huddled around a fire, wearing leather coats and thick wool socks and mittens. It was so cold that any sort of movement was painful.

FROSTBITE

☞ It's Bad Inside, But Outside Is Worse

☞ A Man Could Die Out There

The shelter was cold, but going outside was even worse. There were snow drifts up to 30 feet (9 m) deep and winds so cold they could cause **frostbite** to the fingers and toes or freeze the eyes. The men's clothes froze on them. But they had to go outside to gather firewood or hunt animals for food. One man, John Williams, died from exposure to extreme cold while out hunting.

ICEBOUND!

★ **Passing the Time**

★ **Tensions Grow Through the Winter**

The *Discovery* was stuck in the ice for nearly eight months. Some of the men became sick and could not help in the struggle to find food and firewood. That made others angry. Tension grew between the crew and Hudson, who was worried that there was not enough food for the men to survive the winter.

> " The frog (as loathsome as a toad) was not spared."
> *Abacuk Pricket describes how the crew ate reptiles.*

GOING HUNGRY

+ **Where's the Food?**

In early winter, the crew shot birds such as ducks and geese to eat. When the birds disappeared, Hudson offered money to anyone who killed "beast, fish, or fowl." Pricket said the men even ate moss. Only when the ice melted could they use nets to catch large numbers of fish. By then the crew had only enough food left for two weeks. They were close to starvation.

Meeting and Greeting

Hudson made new friends as he sailed along the east coast and up the Hudson River. But some of the native people living in the region did not welcome the newcomers.

> "They appear to be a friendly people, but have a **great** propensity **to steal**."
> *Hudson on the Algonquians*

First Contact

☛ **Explorers Lose Their Shirts**

☛ **Unprovoked attack on native camp**

The first native people Hudson met were the Penobscot tribe of Maine. Hudson used signs to communicate that he wanted to trade. He exchanged woolen nightshirts, or pajamas, for valuable animal pelts, or furs. But Hudson's crew feared they would be attacked. To prevent this, they armed themselves with muskets. They stole a canoe and attacked the Penobscot camp, where they stole more furs.

CROWDED REGION

★ **Everyone Lives on the River**

★ **Home to Many Peoples**

When the *Discovery* sailed up the Hudson River in 1609, about 10,000 native people lived in communities along the river. They were mainly Mahican, Lenape, and Iroquois. Some welcomed the Europeans, but those who had dealt with Europeans before were more suspicious. They had good reason. Hudson's crew did not treat the native peoples very well.

FALLING OUT

★ **Trading with the Lenape**

★ **Hostages Taken to Ensure Safety**

At first, the Lenape welcomed Hudson. They canoed out to the ship to trade. But the next day the Lenape attacked the crew as they explored. One of Hudson's men was killed. In return, the crew took two Lenape as hostages. The warriors broke a hole in the side of the ship to escape.

> **We kept a good watch for fear of being betrayed by the people."**
> *Robert Juet describes life on the Hudson.*

A WARM WELCOME

+ **Feasting and Fighting**

+ **Both Sides Suspicious of the Other**

As Hudson and his crew sailed farther up the river, they met more people. The Mahican were skilled hunters and fishers and built villages, where they grew crops. The Mahican invited Hudson to a feast with their chief. Hudson's men were careful after the violence they had seen. They tricked some native men into getting drunk to see how they behaved. Even though they had never drunk alcohol before, the Mahican acted with perfect manners.

CRAZY CAT

★ **Fearful Feline Spooks Sailors**

★ **Superstitions at Sea**

As the *Discovery* sailed upriver, the ship's cat panicked and ran from one side of the deck to the other, looking overboard. Robert Juet wrote, "This made us wonder, but we saw nothing." The incident made the crew jumpy, because sailors were very **superstitious**. For instance, they believed cats were lucky and that whistling would make the wind blow.

More Meetings

Hudson's encounters with native people were generally friendly. But when he sailed into Hudson Bay he was sailing into one of the most difficult places in the world to survive.

STAYING APART

+ Explorer Ignored by Locals

+ Campfires Sighted on Shore

Native people often traded with European explorers. They exchanged animal furs for beads and knives. But some did not want anything to do with the newcomers. When he sailed along the edge of James Bay looking for food, Hudson could see the campfires of the Cree on the shore. But only one man made contact with the crew of the *Discovery*. The rest kept their distance.

MEET THE CREE

★ **Survival Experts**

The Cree lived in the harsh landscape of Hudson Bay. To get food they used *tipa-achimowina*, knowledge that had been handed down through generations about how to hunt different animals, where to fish, or where to find berries or seaweed. Hudson Bay had lots of wildlife—if you knew where to find it. For example, the Cree had words for 200 different species of birds, most of which they ate. They also caught fish and hunted mammals.

THE VANISHING MAN

☛ Explorers Startled by Unexpected Visitor

☛ Mystery Guest Fails to Return

Stuck in the ice in James Bay, the crew of the *Discovery* were startled one day when a hunter arrived at their shelter. He was probably Cree. Hudson gave the man a mirror, some buttons, and a knife. The next day the man returned with two deer skins and two beaver pelts to exchange in return for his gifts. But although the man promised to come back with more pelts, he never returned. Cree stories recorded that the explorers even offered to exchange their clothes for the furs the hunter wore.

DEATH ON THE ICE

★ Hunters of the Arctic Circle

★ Fatal Fight Leaves Mutineers Dead

On the way back to England after casting Hudson adrift, the mutineers stopped at Digges Island in Hudson Bay. They met Inuit hunters who seemed friendly. The Inuit showed the sailors how to trap seabirds for food. But when the two groups disagreed about a trade, a fight broke out. The Inuit attacked the men and fired arrows at them as they fled in the ship's boat. Four sailors died, including Henry Greene—who the survivors later said had led the mutiny.

I Love Nature

Did you know?
European sailors described seeing seal-narwhals. The narwhal a long horn, and sailo mistook them for unicorns.

Henry Hudson's explorations brought him and his crew into contact with brand new animals and plants, as well as species with which they were familiar from back home.

PATRIDGE IN A PEAR TREE

- ☛ James Bay on Migration Route
- ☛ Winter Skies Full of Birds

For their first three months in James Bay, the crew of the *Discovery* ate well. They killed 1,200 white partridges and caught fish in the sea. There were also lots of water birds to catch, including snow geese, Canada geese, and many kinds of ducks. As the winter grew colder and the sea froze over, however, the birds headed south to find warmer conditions. The men were left short of food.

TRAVEL UPDATE

Hunters' Paradise

★ Hudson Bay is rich with mammals **adapted** to living in the winter climate of northern Canada. The biggest include moose, elk, and caribou. Smaller animals are rabbits, foxes, porcupines, and even skunks. Out on the ice, seals and walruses bask in the winter sun.

TAMARACK MAGIC

★ **Sticky Buds Used to Make Medicine**

★ **Tastes Horrible—But It Works!**

When the food began to run out in James Bay, the crew began to get sick from **scurvy** and frostbite. They drank medicine made by boiling the buds of a tamarack tree, which is a kind of larch. It tasted so bad the men could barely drink it. The surgeon held hot buds on the men's aching joints, which helped the crew who were sick from the cold.

Medicine

Native people used tamarack bark to make medicine to treat everything from cuts and frostbite to arthritis.

MERMAID AHOY!

☛ **Exotic Creature Spotted Near Ship**

☛ **Half Woman, Half Fish!**

On his second journey, in 1608, Hudson was sailing north of Norway when his crew got a surprise. They spotted what looked like a woman swimming near the ship. She had long, black hair and white skin, but a tail like a porpoise. Books from that time told of strange sea creatures, and many sailors believed in mermaids. But Hudson carefully noted the names of the men who said they had seen the mermaid. He probably wanted to avoid seeming too superstitious himself, in case people did not take his voyages seriously.

GREEN SHOOTS

+ **Green Leaves Prevent Scurvy**

+ **Vitamin C Defeats Disease**

Scurvy was a serious danger faced by sailors in the 17th century. It was a disease caused by a lack of vitamin C in their diets. Sailors could prevent it by eating green leaves. The crew gathered sorrel and "scurvy grass," or spoonwart, from meadows around Hudson Bay. Even though the leaves tasted bitter, the men made sure they ate them.

Fortune Hunting

Hudson's voyages made him famous. If he had survived, he might have become rich. His expeditions opened the way for Europeans to exploit the resources of remote parts of North America.

MERCHANT COMPANIES

☞ Merchants Group Together to Fund Exploration

☞ Vast Fortunes to Be Made Overseas

The organizations that funded most exploration, including Hudson's voyages, were called merchant companies. Merchants in London, Amsterdam, and other European cities formed associations to share the risk of paying for overseas voyages. They got a charter, or permission, from the king or queen to allow them to explore new lands. They wanted to increase their trade by finding new customers or new supplies of resources.

FUR TRADERS

+ Explorer's Failure Makes a Fortune

Fur Trade Thrives in Europe

Hudson failed in his quest to find a route to Asia, but he found something almost as valuable—fur. Fur was in demand in Europe for fashion and to make warm clothes. The English started the Hudson Bay Company to trade for fur pelts with native hunters. French **trappers** killed millions of beaver. Their fur was used to give a silky feel to men's top hats.

THAR SHE BLOWS!

★ **Whalers Head for North Atlantic**

★ **Huge Profits to Be Made**

The North Atlantic was a key hunting ground for whales. The animals produced oil for lamps and a waxy substance called ambergris, used in medicine and perfume. But whales could sink a small ship. When a whale swam beneath the *Discovery* off Greenland, the crew was terrified it would turn the ship over. When it left, they thanked God for sparing their lives.

POWER POLITICS

☛ **The Dutch Take the Lead on the East Coast**

☛ **Settlement Grows Rapidly at Manhattan**

The English and the Dutch both hoped to benefit from Hudson's trips to North America. The Dutch East India Company exploited the territory he claimed along the Hudson River. At its mouth, they bought an island from the native people. It became New Amsterdam. The English later captured the settlement and renamed it New York.

This Isn't What It Said in the Brochure!

Being stuck in James Bay in the wilderness during the harsh winter was bad enough. But when spring came, things got worse for Henry Hudson—much, much worse.

MAKING ENEMIES

> **+ Captain Deaf to Crew's Complaints**

> **+ Tensions Grow During Long Winter**

Henry Hudson was a great navigator, but he was poor at leading his crew. When some men wanted to head home after the winter in James Bay, Hudson refused. He fired Robert Juet as mate and also angered William Wilson, the **boatswain**. When Hudson also refused to give a coat to Henry Greene, Greene decided to get even. When the mutiny began, Greene, Wilson, and Juet were among the ringleaders.

THE MUTINEERS STRIKE

> ☛ **Mutiny in the Arctic**

> ☛ **Captain and Loyal Crewmen Cast Adrift**

On 20 June, 1609, after the *Discovery* was freed from the ice, William Wilson and Henry Greene planned a mutiny. They persuaded Juet and others to join them. The next day, they grabbed Hudson. They forced him and his loyal crewmen into the ship's shallop, or open boat, and cut them adrift.

GONE!

★ **Lost Without a Trace**

★ **Carpenter's Loyalty Costs Him his Life**

Apart from Henry Hudson and his son John, most of the men forced into the boat were sick. But the ship's carpenter, Philip Staffe, was determined to be loyal to his captain, against the wishes of the mutineers. He took his carpenter's chest, an iron pot, and a gun and gunpowder for shooting birds. Perhaps he was able to make the men a shelter and hunt for food—but we will probably never know. After the *Discovery* sailed out of sight, the men in the open boat were never heard from again.

My Explorer Journal

★ **Whose side are you on? Do you think the mutineers had a good reason to do what they did? Or would you have joined the crew who decided to be cast adrift with Hudson? Explain your reasons.**

TRAVEL UPDATE

Cast Adrift!

★ Even at the end of winter, James Bay is no place to be in an open boat. The water is still bitterly cold and the water full of floating ice. The men in the shallop rigged a small sail to follow the *Discovery*, but the big ship left it far behind. Hudson probably decided to try to reach the shore to find shelter for the men who were sick.

End of the Road

The *Discovery*'s voyage home was difficult. More men died on the way. At home, the survivors faced trial for murder—people assumed that Hudson was dead.

FATAL FIGHT

☛ **Homeward Voyage Highly Dangerous**

☛ **Mutineers Fight with Inuit**

The thirteen men left on the *Discovery* sailed for home. A few, led by Henry Greene, wanted to become pirates. They never got the chance. On Digges Island, near the exit of Hudson Bay, they were attacked by Inuit hunters. Henry Greene, William Wilson, and two others were killed as the rest of the crew fled.

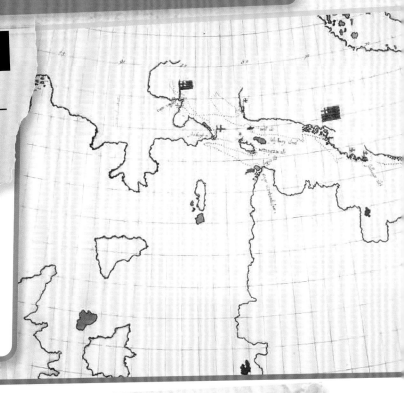

DEAD OR ALIVE?

★ **Who Can Find Hudson?**

★ **Could Anyone Have Survived?**

A number of expeditions set out to rescue Hudson, including one organized by Thomas Smythe, governor of the East India Company. Finally, in 1631 an expedition found what might have been the remains of a hut on an island in James Bay. There was no real proof. Perhaps the men died in the open boat. But stories passed down among the Cree describe bearded men. Perhaps they were the European sailors, living in Cree villages.

GETTING AWAY WITH IT

+ On Trial for their Lives

+ Mutineers Escape the Gallows

★ **Imagine you are a defense lawyer at the trial. Using details of the mutiny in the text, explain to the jury why your clients should not be hanged for overthrowing their captain and leaving him and the others to die.**

The *Discovery* arrived back in London on October 20, 1611. Robert Bylot, who had acted as captain, reported to Thomas Smythe and Hudson's other backers. They wanted the survivors to be tried for murder, but the trial was delayed for seven years. By then Abacuk Pricket had written his account of the voyage. He said the main **conspirators** had been killed by the Inuit. His colleagues agreed. They may have been trying to not take the blame themselves. The court found them not guilty. Some crewmen headed back to the Arctic again. Bylot became a respected explorer in his own right.

DEATH!

The Admiralty was responsible for the law at sea. If the mutineers had been found guilty of murder, they would have been hanged.

GLOSSARY

adapted To have become suited by nature to a situation

blueprints Drawings on paper of a plan for building

boatswain An officer on a ship who is in charge of its sails, ropes, boats, and decks

cast adrift To set someone afloat in a vessel without any way of steering themselves

conspirators Those who plan with others in secret to do some act

exploit To use for economic gain

frostbite A medical condition in which the skin and flesh of parts of the body become swollen and infected from exposure to cold temperatures

horizon A point where the earth meets the sky

inlet A bay or a waterway into a sea, lake, or river

mate An officer who is assistant to a ship's captain

Muslim Follower of the Islamic religion

mutiny A rebellion against someone in authority, especially by a ship's crew against their officers

narwhals Arctic whales; males have one or two long, twisted tusks

navigator Officer responsible for planning and recording the course of a ship's journey

Northeast Passage A water route from the Atlantic Ocean through the Russian Arctic to the Pacific Ocean

Northwest Passage A water route from the Atlantic Ocean through the Canadian Arctic to the Pacific Ocean

propensity A tendency to act in a certain way

scurvy A disease caused by a lack of Vitamin C. Sufferers bleed under their skin and from their gums. Sufferers become weak and can die.

Spice Islands A group of Islands of Indonesia, now known as the Moluccas. Europeans valued the spices grown there which they used to help flavor plain or spoiled food.

strait A narrow channel that connects two larger bodies of water

superstitious To hold an irrational belief that an action or object can influence events with which they in fact have no connection

trapper Someone who traps wild animals for fur

APRIL
Henry Hudson sets out on his first voyage but fails to find a route over the North Pole.

JANUARY
The Dutch East India Company hires Hudson to find the Northeast Passage.

MAY
Blocked by wintry weather, Hudson turns back at North Cape and heads to North America.

SEPTEMBER
Hudson claims the site of present-day New York for the Dutch and begins exploring the Hudson River.

1607 **1608** **1609**

APRIL
Hudson begins his second voyage. He reaches Novaya Zemlya, north of Russia, before turning back.

APRIL
Hudson sets sail on the *Half Moon*.

JULY
Hudson lands at Penobscot Bay and begins to explore the east coast.

ON THE WEB

www.marinersmuseum.org/education/henry-hudson
Biography of Hudson from the Mariners' Museum, Newport, Virginia, America's National Maritime Museum

www.ianchadwick.com/hudson/
A detailed biography of Henry Hudson with timelines of his four voyages

www.pbs.org/empireofthebay/profiles/hudson.html
A page about Hudson to accompany the PBS series *Empire of the Bay*.

www.softschools.com/timelines/henry_hudson_timeline/25/
Timeline of Hudson's life and career

BOOKS

Gleason, Carrie. *Henry Hudson* (In the Footsteps of Explorers). Crabtree Publishing Company, 2005.

Gould, Jane. *Henry Hudson* (Jnr. Graphic Famous Explorers). PowerKids Press, 2013.

Molzhan, Arlene Bourgeois. *Henry Hudson, Explorer of the Hudson River* (Explorers!). Enslow Elementary, 2003.

Petrie, Kristin. *Henry Hudson* (Explorers). Checkerboard Library, 2007.

Smalley, Carol Parenzan. *Henry Hudson* (What's So Great About?). Mitchell Lane Publishers, 2006.

Young, Jeff C. *Henry Hudson: Discoverer of the Hudson River* (Great Explorers of the World). Enslow Publishers, 2009.

DECEMBER
On his return to London, Hudson is arrested by order of the king for sailing for the Dutch.

JUNE
Discovery sails into the "Furious Overfall," now known as Hudson Strait, then on into Hudson Bay.

JUNE 22
Thirteen of the crew mutiny. They put Hudson and eight others in an open boat and cast them adrift.

SEPTEMBER
After a trip during which a man dies of hunger, the crew of *Discovery* arrive in London .

1610

1611

APRIL
Hudson sets sail on his fourth voyage on board *Discovery*, searching for the Northwest Passage.

OCTOBER
After failing to find another exit from Hudson Bay, Hudson and his crew are stuck in the ice in James Bay, where they spend the winter.

JUNE
Discovery is free of the ice. Hudson wants to sail west, but some of the crew want to go home.

JULY
Four mutineers are killed in a clash with Inuit on Digges Island.

INDEX